88 Ideas to Teach More Effectively

C000144838

'This is GOOD. Really, really extraordinary stuff. I don't think I've ever seen a similar book on education.'

– Seth Godin

'Tim writes with flair . . . A book you can read, dip into, come back to, and I can imagine these pages appearing on a student or teacher's desk to inspire, contemplate, or react to.'

– John Hattie

If you are after a compendium of detailed lesson plans, this is not the book for you.

If you want to hear from a self-professed teaching guru, this is not the book for you.

If you believe the road to being an effective teacher is paved with uncertainty, contradictions and mistakes . . . this may be the book for you.

Designed to be unlike any other education book, *88 Ideas to Teach More Effectively* is packed with practical wisdom to encourage teachers to maximise their impact and be happier.

This book aims to challenge and inspire students, teachers and everyone involved in education, no matter what their background. All will find value in reading this concise and accessible book.

Combined with 88 entertaining, full-colour illustrations, this book is basically a chocolate bar that's good for you!

Topics include:

- Hook 'em early;
- Forget being the favourite;
- Teach sticky;
- Say I don't know;
- Teachable moments;
- Removing your emotions;
- You will feel terrible sometimes;
- You're not 'just a teacher';
- Don't miss an opportunity.

88 Ideas to Teach More Effectively is an invaluable guide for students, teachers and newly qualified teachers who want to reflect on their role and impact . . . plus, it has pretty pictures.

Tim Bowman is a classroom teacher, blogger, founder of Class Creator and TEDx speaker. He has taught in local and international schools including in Hong Kong and Australia. He hated his first day teaching, but after thirteen years in a classroom he thinks it's the best job going round.

88 Ideas to Teach More Effectively

Forget being the favourite!

Tim Bowman

Routledge
Taylor & Francis Group

LONDON AND NEW YORK

First published 2017
by Routledge
2 Park Square, Milton Park, Abingdon, Oxon OX14 4RN

and by Routledge
711 Third Avenue, New York, NY 10017

Routledge is an imprint of the Taylor & Francis Group, an informa business

© 2017 Tim Bowman

The right of Tim Bowman to be identified as author of this work has been asserted by him in accordance with sections 77 and 78 of the Copyright, Designs and Patents Act 1988.

All rights reserved. No part of this book may be reprinted or reproduced or utilised in any form or by any electronic, mechanical, or other means, now known or hereafter invented, including photocopying and recording, or in any information storage or retrieval system, without permission in writing from the publishers.

Trademark notice: Product or corporate names may be trademarks or registered trademarks, and are used only for identification and explanation without intent to infringe.

British Library Cataloguing in Publication Data
A catalogue record for this book is available from the British Library

Library of Congress Cataloging in Publication Data
Names: Bowman, Tim, 1979-
Title: 88 ideas to teach more effectively : forget being the favourite! / Tim Bowman.
Other titles: Eighty-eight ideas to teach more effectively.
Description: New York : Routledge, 2017.
Identifiers: LCCN 2016014245| ISBN 9781138675414 (hardback) | ISBN 9781138675421 (pbk.) | ISBN 9781315560717 (ebook)
Subjects: LCSH: Teaching.
Classification: LCC LB1025.3 .B687 2017 | DDC 371.102--dc23LC record available at https://lccn.loc.gov/2016014245

ISBN: 978-1-138-67541-4 (hbk)
ISBN: 978-1-138-67542-1 (pbk)
ISBN: 978-1-315-56071-7 (ebk)

Typeset in DIN by
Servis Filmsetting Ltd, Stockport, Cheshire

Introduction

This is *not* a book about things I do well.

This is *not* a book of things I have "discovered".

This book is *not* an in-depth "deep dive" into pedagogy.

This book is designed to be easily consumed by busy teachers.

I hope this book is on the right side of the fine line between synced and vague.

The book is about things I have learned from the many great teachers I have worked with.

It is filled with contradictions, highlighting perhaps how teaching is both an art and a science.

I hope you enjoy it and, most important, find it valuable.

Cheers,
Tim Bowman
Teacher, author, speaker, founder of Class Creator (www.classcreator.io), husband and father.
www.facebook.com/88ideasteaching/

PS: I love getting in touch with authors of books I've read. So if you're the same, please feel free to contact me at tim@classcreator.io

Foreword by Professor John Hattie

Chair, Board of the Australian Institute for Teaching and School Leadership.
Associate Director of the ARC-SRI: Science of Learning Research Centre.
Author of *Visible Learning*, *Visible Learning for Teachers* and more.

It is exciting to write a book, more exciting to have people read it, ecstasy when some tell you they enjoyed it, but the ultimate is to have an innovative interpretation. This book tells much of my Visible Learning story in pictures, comments, high levels of wit, and prompts many challenges. It adds much more and the competence of Tim is exhibited throughout.

I write "academese", Tim writes with flair. Consider some of the headlines and it is so inviting: Say "I don't know"; Teach sticky; Beware of your strengths; The bank; Be in their corner; Not all noise is created equal.

A book you can read, dip into, come back to, and I can imagine these pages appearing on a student's or teacher's desk to inspire, contemplate, or react to.

The underlying messages are worth re-examining and I invite you to read via the pictures and words. It is about inspired, passionate and impact teaching; it asks us to consider our impact on students and reminds that the learning of the student is the reason we are all in this business. And this learning impact will increase if we too are learning, re-interpreting, and examining our influences.

As Socrates proclaimed, an unexamined life is not worth living, and Tim asks about what is worthwhile in our schools, and suggests that if we, as educators, fail to question our influence then we may not be deserving of the powerful and influential position we have.

Enjoy.

Acknowledgments

This book had been swimming in my head for many years. In mid-2014 I shared some of the ideas with a few people and they liked it, so I set up a KickStarter campaign to see if others would like it. I was overwhelmed by the support and generosity of fifty-seven "backers". To them . . . thank you.

Lesley Davies, Julie Markie, Briony McKelson, Ronnie J., Tamas Kassay, John Hewat, David King, Candice Hickey, Ale Mohamad, Brian Paxton, Matt Scott, Daniel Bryant, Lee Gan, Catherine Twomey, Toby Daniel, Mark McKelson, Craig Bloxsome, Peter Hartman, Chris Killen, Jennifer Lemon, Mia Sharman, Cameron Hunter, M. Dreier, Debbie Woods, Rob Graham, Cayla Sivell, J. Brady, Daniel J. Peters, Riahna, Jenny Johnson, Heather Sharps, Dave Brown, Mitch Smith, Antonia McKenzie, Paul Hay, Linda Quinton, James Kassay, Mel Paxton, Pat 'n' John Brookfield, Janice Jensen, Ray Heathcote, Tim Tremmel, Michelle Sarjana, Timothy Luck, Gillian Noonan, Leese Duff, Kharma Greer, Linda Amos, Sure Robertson, Kaye Seton, Gary Methven, Ali Groh, Andrew Horsburgh, Jeremy Ta'kody, Michael Davies, Emily Booth, Ross Dawson, Nick Millar, Matthew Key, Lisa Kidd, Jenn Roberts, Di Brummelen, Chantelle Brown, Joe Dannaoui, Jenny Anderson, John Twist, Shane Davey, and many many more.

Thank you to my parents for "encouraging" me to try teaching, even when I didn't get into university and I had to weasel my way in via the backdoor. You are the greatest teachers I'll ever have.

Thank you to my in-laws for your constant support and friendship.

Thank you to all the teachers I have worked with, especially the amazing ones who taught me how to teach and helped me love the career.

Thank you to the great teachers I had as a kid. You made learning fun, and inspired me to inspire others.

Thank you to all the teachers out there that go above and beyond to make the world a better place. You are more important than you will ever know. Keep it up!

Thank you to all those amazing "teachers" in my life who aren't teachers. The coaches, mentors, friends, authors and weirdos that have shown me a better way to do things.

Thank you to the team at Routledge for your support, understanding and experience. Bruce Roberts and Sarah Richardson, you guys rock!

Thank you to my wife, Corinne. You are my greatest supporter, my best friend and my one true love.

Images used in this book are Creatives Commons images from:

Gratisography – http://gratisography.com/
Pexels – http://www.pexels.com/
Pixabay – https://pixabay.com/

Images are Creative Commons Zero and donations have been made to the sites as a "thank you".

FORGET BEING THE FAVOURITE

It's easy to get your students to love you.

Give them chocolate and free time, and you will be *"my favourite teacher ever"*.

Aim higher.

Aim to be the *best* teacher a kid ever had.

The teacher who sees something in the student that the student may not see in themselves.

Be the teacher who encourages students to dream big, try, fail, learn from the experience and go again.

Being respected trumps being liked.

HOOK 'EM EARLY

Give your students something different.

Make their heads explode, or at least spin.

Do something unexpected, exciting and engaging.

You can't do it all the time, but try to do it as early and often as possible.

For me, I like to set fire to or smash something as early as possible in the school year.

The kids love it and are hooked.

Many, if not most, students see education as a routine, often a boring one, so by doing something different, you wake them from their educational slumber.

SAY "I DON'T KNOW"

Say it often.

Say it because you are comfortable not knowing everything.

But more importantly, say it because it allows your students to say it.

You do not have to know *everything* to be a teacher.

The sooner a teacher gets comfortable NOT being the smartest person in the room, the better off they and their students are.

Say it, even when you do know the answer to get students thinking for themselves.

"I don't know; *what do you think*?"

"I don't know; *how could we find out*?"

You are selling all day.

You have a captive market; they are trapped in your classroom, but they *do not have to buy*.

You are selling learning, and your students pay with their attention.

Many of them are savvy buyers used to instant gratification.

Some have even tried to buy into learning before and failed, so why should they buy in again?

Like it or not, you are a "salesman".

If your students aren't buying, you have to change your sales pitch.

Teachers can no longer expect students to "do their job and engage".

For better or worse, those days are long gone.

Great salespeople find out about their customers and then demonstrate how their product will make the life of the customer better.

Great teachers "sell" to students by engaging their students and showing the value of the learning.

WIIFM

"What's in it for me?"

This is very much related to being a salesperson.

If you want your students to pay you attention, you have to demonstrate to them "what's in it for them".

As teachers, we can't assume students know "what's in it for them". After all, they don't know what they don't know.

I tell kids they are learning persuasive writing so they can convince their parents to buy them a mobile phone for their next birthday or so they can convince the person they have a crush on to go out with them.

The two worst reasons to pay attention that kids hear all the time:

1. It will be on the test (tests do not motivate all students, or even most).
2. You'll need it for your job (too far away).

Make sure the thing "in it for them" is something they'll want now, not in twenty years.

Are you really interested in your superannuation fund? No. Of course you aren't because the payoff is too far away.

Make the pay off now and something they care about.

TEACH STICKY

I taught my class the concept of food chains in grade four.

Two years later, I taught the same kids in grade six.

They had forgotten everything I had taught them . . . and they were really smart kids.

I hadn't taught sticky.

Sticky is a term given to an idea that attaches itself to someone.

It's used in marketing, and it should be used in teaching.

Teachers should aim to teach so it stays with students for life . . . like chewing gum under the table in a restaurant.

To be sticky, your idea has to be interesting and meaningful to students.

Ideally, learning then becomes an emotional experience.

PAY NOW OR PAY LATER

The way I look at it, at some stage you are going to have to work:

Before the lesson – to plan a great, engaging and well-managed lesson,

or

During the lesson – to manage a bunch of students who are not engaged with the lesson.

Personally, I'd rather work hard on the planning and enjoy the teaching.

Pay in your planning, or pay in front of your class, it's up to you.

GET REAL

Whenever possible, bring the real world into the classroom.

Bring real world experiences into the classroom.

Whether it is negotiating for a car, writing an ad to sell a hair dryer on eBay or figuring out which packet of chocolate offers the best value at the supermarket, all these scenarios are useful for demonstrating how skills learnt at school are useful in the real world.

Students love learning about addition/subtraction by figuring out which one of their favourite celebrities earned the most money last year making movies.

They enjoy learning about money by selling ice lollies at lunchtime, calculating a float, keeping inventory and recording profits. They like learning to write by composing a letter to the principal pleading for a plug for the interactive whiteboard.

One of my favourite real investigations: Why does a football made in our country cost $30/£15, while a football made in India and shipped 7,000km to us only cost $12/£6?

GETTING IT WRONG

I once brought a lesson from the world into the classroom.

It was a really interesting news article about the changing state of the tomato market and how foreign production of tomatoes was affecting the local growers.

Tomato growers . . . what was I thinking?

Yep, it was interesting **to me**.

The kids really couldn't care less about the state of the tomato market.

I'd completely mistaken *my* interest for *theirs*.

Make sure the "real world" has a relationship to *their real world*, not just yours.

NO WRITTEN WORD...

No written word, no spoken plea, can teach our youth what they should be.
Nor all the books on all the shelves. It's what the teachers are themselves.

- Be a risk-taker.
- Be caring.
- Be in love with learning.
- Be reflective.
- Be awesome.

Every second of every day you are modelling your expectations of your students.

Be the person you want your students to be.

Shut the door on the ancient teachers' mantra, "Do as I say, not as I do".

If you want your students to love learning, be respectful and self-motivate. The best way to ensure this is to demonstrate how you are respectful, self-motivated and love learning.

Our actions will teach our students far more than our words ever will.

GIVE THEM OPTIONS

We all love to think it was "our idea", and kids are no different.

Offering kids a choice gives them a sense of ownership.

"Would you like to do X or Z?" is far better than, "Today you have to do X".

If you want them to do "X", give them an option "Z", but make it really unattractive.

Once again this is a tactic salespeople use. It's called an Alternative Close. They won't ask, "So, do you think you will buy the car?" They ask, "Would you like your new car in blue or red?"

THE 4 F'S

Firm
Firm doesn't mean being nasty or a bully.

It means setting expectations, with positive and negative consequences, and following through.

Fair
Kids expect justice in a classroom.

It is also important to explain that "fairness" does not mean "the same for everyone".

Fairness is about giving everyone what they need and deserve.

Friendly
You don't need to be the kids' best friend; just show them respect and be nice to them.

Ask them questions about their lives.

Pay them a compliment about who they are.

Find out who they feel they are (golfer, dancer, maths geek, cook, etc.) and help nurture that sense of self.

Feedback
Ask your kids for respectful feedback.

"Was that lesson engaging?"
"How could I have done that better?"
"I'm thinking we could do it A or B way; which do you think is best?"
"Is that fair?"

27

DEALING WITH PARENTS

Generally, parents want two things:

To be heard.
Whenever dealing with a parent, let them get their point of view out.

Don't try to jump in with answers or excuses or become defensive/aggressive.

Be an active listener. Nod.

Ask gentle questions to clarify your understanding.

Let them get out what they need to, so they feel heard.

To be listened to.
Then show you have listened.

Offer an action plan, ask their advice, tell them you will follow it up and get back to them, thank them for bringing it to your attention.

Show you have heard and listened to them, and you will be far more likely to nurture a positive relationship.

STRUCTURE

As adults, most of the time when we are nervous it is because we are uncertain about the future. It's the same for students. Kids like structure . . . as it leads to security.

Structure doesn't mean a long list of rules or doing the same thing, the same way, every day.

It means reasonably predictable cause and effect. Consistency.

Does your classroom have a structure?

Could your students predict how you would react to most situations?

It is a great idea to talk about what is ahead in the session, day, week, term or year.

It engages students on what to look for, and for many students it provides a much needed sense of security.

PARENTS ARE ... PASSIONATE
(MY PUBLISHER WOULDN'T LET ME USE THE WORD PSYCHOS)

Parents are psychos . . . I should know, I'm one of them.

One day you may be a parent, and then you will understand why parents are psychos.

I used to think I cared for my students as much as their parents . . . then I had my own child.

A good parent will stop at nothing for their child.

That doesn't mean they are right, and it certainly doesn't excuse poor parent behaviour, but it does explain their passion.

The best way to deal with this is to show them you are aligned with them.

"You're obviously really concerned about this and so am I. All I want is the best outcome for Tim. How can we work together to make that happen?"

REVERSE ENGINEER

Reverse engineer your teaching.

Think of the finished product.

What would success look like?

What do you want your kids to learn?

Why do you want them to learn it?

How is it going to help them? What's in it for them (short term)?

What is the best way to help them learn it?

It sounds simple, but it's amazing how many teachers "teach something" without reflecting on the why and how to do it best.

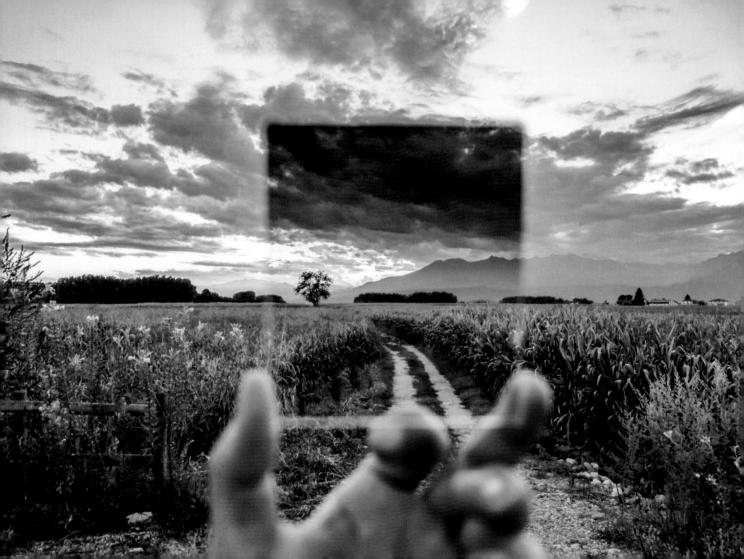

STUDENTS' POINT OF VIEW

Try and see things from the point of view of your students . . . literally.

- Sit in their seats.
- Line up where they line up.
- Do their work.
- Do their homework.
- Go into their toilets (best when students aren't there); often, they are disgusting.

What sort of headspace would going to the toilet put your students in?

What do you see and feel?

Do you want to feel what it is like to have a learning difficulty?

Try writing "abacus" as a mirror image . . . with your non-preferred hand.

Much slower? Messy? Remind you of any kids in your class?

YOUR WEAKNESS CAN BE YOUR STRENGTH

I am dyslexic.

As a kid, I hated reading.

I was terrified of reading aloud because I would undoubtedly make a mistake.

Jump forward fifteen years, and as a teacher, my school reports are a proofreader's nightmare, and I undoubtedly miss heaps of mistakes that my students make.

But I think my weakness is also my strength.

I can empathise with students who hate reading.

I understand they don't hate reading . . . They hate the experience of public failure that many teachers have never experienced.

If you have an Achilles heel, it will likely make you more sensitive to the Achilles heel of others. Your experiences and personal challenges can make you the champion a student needs.

BEWARE OF YOUR STRENGTHS

I've got a strong "teacher voice and stare" that gets results (usually).

It's very easy for me to fall back on my voice, especially when I'm tired or time poor.

As a result, I've used my voice to deal with situations that didn't require it.

As time poor teachers we often use a hammer (big voice, detention, etc.) to solve a problem that would be better served by using a pair of tweezers.

If you can take a few extra breaths to determine what your minimal response should be, your students will trust and respect you more.

TREAT THE CAUSE, NOT THE SYMPTOM

Where possible, dig under the "what" to find and deal with the "why".

For example, a student calls the person he sits next to "gay".

One way to solve this is to change the kids' seating arrangements. This often solves the teacher's problem, but not the kids'. The harassed student will still be vulnerable in the playground, on the way home and, nowadays, online.

Where possible, take the time to get to the cause of the problem and try to resolve it. It's not always easy to do . . . but no one said teaching was going to be easy. If you don't have time now, make a note and be sure to come back to it.

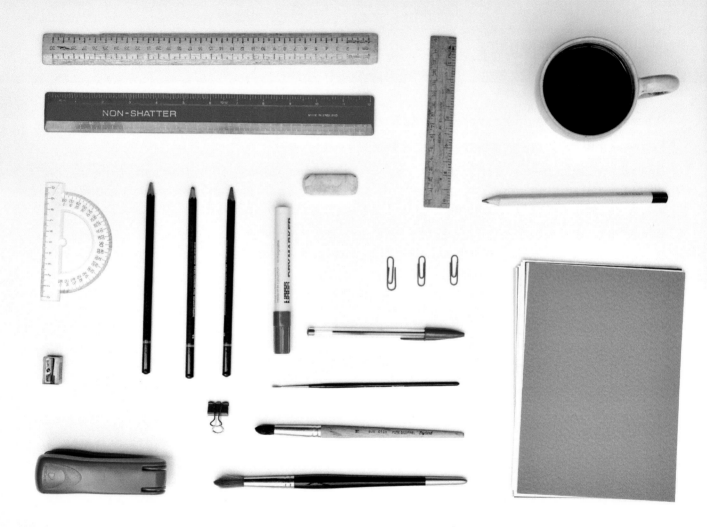

USE YOUR SUPERPOWER

If my students are bored, I speak in an accent.

It re-engages them instantly.

Not everyone can, or would want to, speak in an accent, but the point is, use whatever your strengths are.

If you've got many "superpowers", use them all.

- Sense of humour
- Organised
- Designer
- Artsy
- Musical
- Sporty
- Knowledgeable
- Caring
- Computer geek
- You know the words to all the One Direction songs.

Whatever you've got, and everyone has something, use it.

DON'T REINVENT THE WHEEL, BUT MAKE SURE IT FITS

When I was a kid, all worksheets were handmade . . . not hand-typed . . . handmade.

Therefore, everything was custom built to suit the needs of the teacher's students (theoretically).

Nowadays, you don't have to reinvent the wheel. There are a ridiculous number of educational resources online.

The catch is, if you use these resources without thought or alterations, they are almost always destined to fail.

"One size fits all" is not a term that applies to education.

Also, when you have ownership of the lesson, even by making adjustments to someone else's plan, it takes on a new strength that students can sense. Hunt out ideas, resources and inspiration, but don't grab something off the Internet and use it without making it personal and relevant to your students.

TEACHER "BANK ACCOUNT"

Teachers have "bank accounts" with their students.

Like any bank account, the teacher/student bank account can be in credit (good) or debit (bad).

Grow your bank account by showing your students you value and respect them.

Put in extra effort to make a lesson awesome, rather than photocopying a page from a text book.

Ask them, and respect their opinion. Go and watch a student's soccer game or dance concert or play a ball game with them at lunchtime.

Your capital will go through the roof, and you'll all benefit from that.

Don't waste your capital on small things.

Only call for your students' attention when you really need it.

Try not to pick "fights" that aren't worth having.

Let the little things go.

When you make a mistake, own up to it and pay the capital back with an apology.

STUDENT "BANK ACCOUNT"

Give all students a clean slate, but let them know their actions affect your opinion of them.

This is something you must discuss with students so they understand that everyone is treated the same way, *but* everyone has a different history.

I describe it like how the police give points for driving offences. The bigger the offence, the more points are given. The more offences that occur, the greater the chance the person will lose his or her licence or end up in jail.

Make efforts to keep kids in the credit. Sometimes you might surround them with positive influences or you might focus on the positives while "not seeing" the negatives. Other times, you might put them on a payment/behaviour plan.

JUDGING A STUDENT BY HIS/HER COVER

This will likely be obvious to most, but I've made the mistake before . . . more than once: assuming a kid is, or is not, intelligent because of how he or she appears.

The kids who answer questions aren't necessarily smarter than those who don't.

Very often, it's quite the opposite.

Some students love attention; others prefer to cruise under the radar.

Quieter kids may listen, absorb and reflect more.

The same principle applies to assuming a kid isn't bright academically because he does silly things socially, listens to bad music and rides a motorbike.

SIMPLIFY

"If you have more than three priorities, you don't have any."

This applies to everything in life.

If you're doing too many things, you generally won't do any of them well.

As teachers, we usually have a million and one things on our plate.

You will be pulled in more directions than three normal people could handle and unless you are superhuman you can't do it all.

I suggest you do things in the following order of priority:

1. Do the things that keep you out of trouble.
2. Do the things that have the greatest impact on your students.
3. Do the things that make life easier.
4. Do anything that's left.

RISK VS. REWARD

Walking into a lion enclosure for fun.

>Risk = Being eaten alive.
>Reward = Looking "cool".

Most people wouldn't walk into the enclosure.

Walking into a lion enclosure to save the person you love most.

>Risk = Being eaten alive.
>Reward = Saving the person you love most.

Most people would RUN into the enclosure.

As teachers our goal should always be to **increase reward** and **decrease risk** for our students so they see value in "having a go". Regularly do a self-audit of your classroom for risk vs reward.

Increase reward:

- Give praise not just for achievement, but also for effort and progress. If students think the only way to receive praise is by being perfect/knowing, many will be scared off "having a go".
- Both intrinsic and extrinsic rewards have their place. I often use extrinsic rewards to motivate students, while they learn about the value of intrinsic rewards. The key to sustainable, long-term success in education relies on students transitioning from intrinsic to extrinsic rewards.

Decrease risk:

- Create an environment where "having a go" is more important than the result. Where mistakes are accepted, and expected, on the path to knowledge.
- Come down hard on any comments that are negative towards a student who has a go and "fails". (I hate the "fail" culture I see developing, whereby it is trendier to call out the shortcomings of others rather than applaud them for having a go.)
- Model everything! Share your learning journey, including feelings of uncertainty, mistakes, struggle and growth.

EMAILS

Try and write brief ones; or people won't read them.

No one has time to read long-winded emails . . . I bet you know someone that you'd like to read this. ☺

Make sure you:

- Read over emails, *as if you are the person receiving it*, before you send it. #empathy
- Edit out things that are not integral to your message. This shows you value the reader's time and the message you are sending is important.
- Use bullet points/lists (easier to read).

Bold any actions you require the person receiving the email to take.

WIN : WIN

I once saw a kid standing outside a classroom that was separated from the corridor by a glass wall.

The kid was leaning with his back against the glass wall, while he tapped his fingers on the glass distracting everyone inside and visibly annoying the teacher who had sent him out of the class.

It was a pretty awesome "middle finger" to the teacher.

It was a near perfect example of the all-too-common adversarial relationship teachers foster in classrooms.

Aim to teach as "us/team", rather than "me vs. you".

Explain your objectives and listen to theirs.

Try to find a common ground where everyone benefits.

Win : Win

CLASSROOM GOALS IN ORDER

The order in my classroom goes:

1. Safety
Kids need to feel safe, physically and emotionally.

There is no negotiation here.

2. Education
Most people would say a teacher's main "thing to do" is to get the kids learning. This remains true even though our mandate for teaching has grown much larger than reading, writing and arithmetic.

3. Fun
I tell my kids, "If you take care of the first two (safety and a commitment to learn), I'll try and take care of the third (fun)."

These are *my* three goals that I share explicitly with my students. You can use them, but I recommend you come up with your own and share them with your students.

GIVE A DOG A NAME

"Oh, you're a Smith? You're not Jason Smith's brother, are you?"

Think about the positive and negative ways this statement could be said.

Then think about the effect each would have on the student it was referring to.

If you label a kid negatively, odds are they will live up to it.

In their mind, they think you've made up your mind about them already, so why would they bother trying to change it.

On the flip-side, if you can take a "naughty kid" and relabel him something else (artistic, clever, funny, die-hard LA Lakers fan, whatever), you are far more likely to win him over . . . and you could completely change his own sense of self-worth.

DON'T LOVE KIDS? DON'T TEACH

It's pretty simple.

You've gotta love working with your students.

Not all the time, but 80 per cent of the time.

There will likely be times you downright loathe the profession, but on the whole, you should love it.

If you don't, think about finding another job because teaching is too important a job to be done by someone who doesn't enjoy it.

If I was a principal I'd ask every interviewee, "If you could do any job, what would it be?" If the interviewee can reel off three+ jobs without even thinking, then it is a bad sign.

YOU WILL FEEL LIKE CRAP SOMETIMES/
YOU WILL WANT TO QUIT SOMETIMES

I'll never forget my first day as a teacher . . . I hated it.

A student, Beyoncé Gaga (not her real name), was being naughty, so I made her sit in the corner. Not great classroom management, but it was my first day.

Then . . . Beyoncé started doing a handstand, and the class erupted in laughter.

OMG! They didn't teach me how to deal with this in university. *This is not the job for me,* I thought.

My first year, I probably thought, *I'm not cut out for this teaching business. Maybe I should do something else*, every week.

Second year, maybe once a month.

Third, probably every second month.

Fourth onwards, it was probably "only" once every three months.

If you feel like this, I believe it's because you are reflective (good) and you care about what you do (very good).

Eat a block of chocolate.

Vent to a friend.

Then get back on the horse!

BE IN THEIR CORNER

I let my students know that they matter to me. They aren't my kids, but they are important people in my life. I like my students to know that I'm there for them when they need me and that I'll be in their corner for any fight they go into.

That doesn't mean I'll agree with them. It doesn't mean I'll fight the fight for them or try to get them out of trouble if they have done wrong. It simply means I will try to ensure they will have someone on their side. For many students having someone "on their side" might be a unique experience, inside or outside of school.

GIVE HONEST PRAISE *WHEN IT'S EARNED*

Teachers that feed students fake praise quickly find that their feedback becomes white noise.

If you fake it, and they pick up on it, your words become meaningless from then on.

Make all feedback honest.

Don't be harsh; always look for the positive, but be real.

Make sure students earn praise or they won't value it.

If you praise their 50 per cent . . . that's all you can expect to get.

Be tactful, respectful and kind . . . but more importantly, be honest.

Kids have a decent "this person is full of it" detector, so they know when you're faking it.

BE AWARE OF YOUR "TEACHING BAGGAGE"

We all teach in different ways.

We bring our experiences, good and bad, into our classrooms.

I often have more patience for boys who struggle to fit in with school academically because I empathise with them.

I also have an unfair distrust of cool "alpha" kids, because as an uncool kid growing up, the cool kids weren't very nice.

That is *my* baggage.

I have to remind myself that the cool kids can be just as nice as us dorks . . . and vice versa.

Some teachers teach soft because their parents were "too hard".

Some teachers teach aggressively because that's how they were taught and "I turned out all right".

Be mindful of why you teach the way you do.

SHHHHHHHH THE "SHHH"

If you are saying "shhh" twenty times an hour, it's time to get a new system.

Use the old hand in the air/claps/a bell/noise thermometer, whatever.

Then have consequences if the noise level gets to be too much. I've seen teachers use "shhh" a hundred plus times . . . in an hour.

If a teacher keeps doing something that doesn't work it undermines their authority.

If it doesn't work, it doesn't work. Try something else.

> *Insanity: doing the same thing over and over again and expecting different results.*
>
> Albert Einstein

SHHHHHHH

Talk less.

Learn to get your point across with fewer words, and your students will listen more.

Challenge yourself to be succinct.

"I will explain this in under one minute or you can eat my lunch."

"Someone time me, my goal is to explain this in less than 88 seconds."

HIGH EXPECTATIONS

"If you let them enter like a herd of elephants, they'll behave like a herd of elephants."

Set clear expectations early.

Plan your expectations and know how you're going to implement them.

As far as classroom management goes, everyone knows, "It's much harder to get them back than to let them go."

If my students enter the classroom in a way I think is inappropriate, I ask them to go out and enter the classroom correctly.

Obviously, you have to alter this to suit your kids and the behaviour they are capable of, but pitch to their BEST behaviour, and don't settle for their worst.

CONSEQUENCES (POSITIVE OR NEGATIVE)

Follow through – We must follow through, or our credibility crumbles. Very important.

Set them well before you need them – This removes the emotion from the equation and lets students know the boundaries. Set them with students and they are far more likely to understand them and see them as fair.

Start small – There isn't much room to raise the stakes from "Stop doing that or you will be expelled".

Be fair – Avoid taking away something the students have been working towards all day, week, term or year. If you do, you run the risk that they'll never work for such things again because they know you could just take it away.

Don't make learning the punishment – "If you keep this up, we'll go back to the classroom and do reading/writing" is a sure-fire way to make kids see reading/writing as an unattractive and boring task.

They need to feel a consequence – Positive consequences should feel great; negative ones should "hurt".

Explain the reason – Explain your intention and reason for any consequence. Positive or negative.

THE MEDICI EFFECT

"The Medici Effect" refers to being open to transferring knowledge from different fields, e.g., from business to education.

Education is excellent at being reflective and looking inwards, but very rarely does it seem to draw from other fields.

Constantly be on the lookout for things you could use in your classroom.

It might be how a maître d' at a restaurant meets her customers, how a salesperson sells his product, how a doctor uses a metaphor to explain a complex idea or how a computer game motivates its players.

Having an open mind to ways those outside of education engage and educate is very valuable.

OVER ENGAGEMENT?

I love engaging students.

I love trying to make them love learning.

At the same time, I feel we can't seek to engage them every minute of every day.

As educators, we are facing an uphill battle against video games and "trophies for getting out of bed".

While running the risk of sounding like a grumpy old man, kids need to learn to be self-disciplined and focused in the face of things they don't like.

I'm not saying to design unengaging lessons, but I am suggesting that you cut yourself some slack sometimes and expect students to apply themselves.

Students also need to learn to adapt – to knuckle down and apply themselves to something that doesn't excite them.

REMOVING YOUR EMOTIONS

Think about the worst decisions you've made in your life.

I'm willing to bet most of them were made when you were in a state of anger, frustration or fear.

The same thing applies in teaching.

Generally, the worst decisions in teaching, the ones that get teachers in trouble or fired, occur at times of high emotion.

Try to be aware of your emotions, and dial it down before you make any threats, promises or decisions.

It's hard, but take a "deep breath", and you will make better decisions.

NOT ALL NOISE IS CREATED EQUAL

Thankfully, the days of "children should be seen and not heard" are behind us, but some teachers still believe classrooms should be monasteries.

Mix it up.

Accept, that often, the best learning requires noise.

But when quiet is required, when you or a student is sharing with the class, there should be no exceptions.

This comes back to setting high expectations and manners.

SAY WHAT YOU WANT, *NOT* WHAT YOU DON'T WANT

"Go to the toilets and come back quickly."

vs.

"When you go to the toilets, don't stop off at the playground and have a swing."

"Stop slouching." vs. "Please sit up."

It's much better to tell kids the behaviour and attitudes you want them to display, rather than harp on about what you don't want.

Right now . . . take one second . . . and . . . don't think about chocolate.

Probably thinking about chocolate, right?

Plant the seed of what you want, not what you don't want.

BEWARE THE "SILVER BULLET"

International Baccalaureate.
National Curriculum.
Common Core.
Inquiry Based Learning.
Explicit Teaching.

Curriculum and educational initiatives change.

Each one fixes the last . . . and creates new problems.

Avoid the zealots that believe there is only one way to teach, and do not let curriculums blinker your teaching.

Think of curriculums as "strings to your bow", each one building strengths, and then pick and choose what *you* think works best for your students.

No Work 4 Work's Sake

Avoid "filler work".

If students master a task, do not give them another ten of the same thing.

Extend them. Extension is awesome; filler is not.

Many teachers feel the need to always keep kids busy, as if they are failing if their students have finished and they don't have something to go on with.

What is so wrong with someone doing a good job, completing a task and then being rewarded with a bit of downtime?

You don't want to punish those who struggle, but at the same time, you don't want to punish those who accomplish a task with ease.

Value your students' time or give it back to them.

They will respect and trust you far more.

BEHIND THE SCENES

For those of us who had a great childhood, we were lucky.

Many, many kids aren't so fortunate.

As kids walk through the classroom door in the morning, their parents may have been having a screaming match in the car on their way to school.

Their dog might have passed away.

Grandma might be sick.

Their sibling might have been tormenting them.

Anything could be going on in their lives.

As much as possible, aim to be the rock, the constant, that many students need.

NICKNAMES

I love them, but I know others hate them.

I give all my students nicknames because I feel it creates a team or family environment.

My students often wear their nickname as a "badge of honour" and mention it years later when I bump into them.

Three rules apply to giving nicknames:

- The nickname must **build a student up**, and never put them down.
- The student has **veto power** over any name. If at any stage the nickname isn't liked by the student, it is scrapped and a new nickname is assigned in its place.
- If a kid doesn't want a nickname, they **don't have to have one**.

STUDENTS MIRROR TEACHERS

This is certainly not true all the time, but definitely sometimes.

Students mirror their teachers.

Noisy teacher often equals noisy students.

Proactive teacher equals proactive students.

Miserable teacher equals miserable students.

Disorganised teacher equals disorganised students.

Reflective teacher equals reflective students.

If you want your students to be more XYZ, think how you could model being more XYZ.

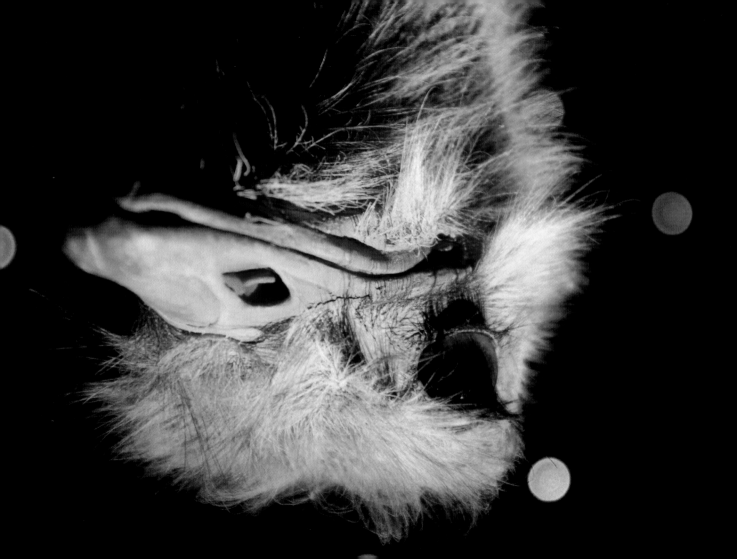

EFFECTIVE VS. EFFICIENT

I have seen great teachers get a concept across to students in far less time than others.

Both were effective, but one was more efficient than the other.

Being effective is about doing the right things, while being efficient is about doing the right things the right way.

One of our greatest challenges as teachers is "fitting everything in".

Focusing on being efficient, doing things faster and just as well, is becoming more important.

This might mean incorporating technology or ditching technology in favour of a more efficient "old school" method.

The key question that should be asked is, "Can we do this a better way?"

BUILD A BRIDGE

In the first week of the year I aim to find out as much as possible about my students as soon as possible.

What makes them tick?

What do they love?

Horses, motocross, Miami Heat, 1820s film noir posters?

Everyone has a passion for something.

I then use that knowledge to build a bridge and establish a common interest.

If I know nothing about their interest, I don't fake it.

I express a genuine interest in understanding and appreciating their interest.

Often it takes time, so don't try to rush building a bridge, but always be searching for an opportunity. It will pay massive dividends down the track.

I put a lot of thought into my start/introduction/first week. My goal is to learn as much about my students as possible. Discovering what motivates and engages each of your students should be priority number one!

WHATEVER FLOATS *THEIR* BOAT

It is very important to always respect your students' identity.

By that, I mean respect their passions, even if you think they are ridiculous.

I learnt this from a TED talk that was saying how poorly video game players are viewed by teachers.

I realised I was disrespecting my video game obsessed students because I wasn't interested in video games.

I thought they were wasting their time. (FYI: I played a lot of video games when I was a kid . . . We all get old and cranky.)

I realised how I was inadvertently building a wall between myself and those students.

The same applies to anything from Justin Bieber to the Collingwood Football Club.

You don't have to like it, but you must respect it.

YOU WILL MAKE MISTAKES

I've made some shockers . . .

I've been rude.
I've been insensitive.
I've been stupid.
I've been a bully.
I've been too loud.
I've been too quiet.
I've said too much.
I've said too little.
I've been too . . . most things.
I've even hit kids (it was an accident).

I didn't want to be any of these at the time, but I was.

Try not to beat yourself up for your mistakes because you will make a lot . . . or you'll be about as interesting as a wall of drying paint.

Learn from your mistakes and try not to do them again . . . although you probably will if I'm anything to go by.

SOMETIMES IT'S EASIER TO ASK FORGIVENESS THAN PERMISSION

Live by this, and you will probably get in trouble . . . but, you could also be awesome.

In teaching, there is a lot of red tape, boxes to be ticked and rules.

"Rules prevent disaster, but often ensure mediocrity." – Barry Schwartz

Sometimes it's easier to jump in and apologise later.

Try not to let the giant bureaucratic rulebook of the education world destroy teaching and learning.

Don't be stupid though!

Rules are often there for a reason.

Weigh up a situation and take some risks, if you think they are worth it. The consequences, if things go wrong, are not earth shattering.

WHAT DO KIDS REALLY NEED TO KNOW?

I feel if my students can walk out of the room with the following three attributes, they'll be ready to take on the world. Feel free to come up with your own and teach to them.

Empathy
Students will understand, care for and be more tolerant of others. They will also be better communicators and problem solvers.

Self discipline
Students will learn to hold themselves accountable and not take the "easy path".

The process of effort, learning and achievement
By learning the process of effort, learning and achievement, students gain the keys to achieving anything. Importantly, they also learn to be comfortable not knowing, so they won't freak out when facing an unfamiliar challenge.

What do you think are the most important things for your students to know?

The students that need you most often are the ones that are the worst at asking for your help.

The correlation between academic success and challenging behaviour is obvious.

The kids that play up or are disengaged are often the ones that need our help most.

Working with these students is when we earn our paycheck and self-respect.

Next time a kid is really testing you, try to stop for a second and reframe their behaviour as a plea for help.

They might need boundaries, or they might need someone to have faith in them . . . but they definitely need something from you at that moment.

DON'T LET "THEM" BRING YOU DOWN

"I want to change the world."

"Ha ha ha, good luck with that!"

There are many supportive and inspirational people that work in education.

But, as in any field, there are also a lot of negative dream-crushers.

The best thing a teacher can do is surround him- or herself with the inspirational ones and prove the dream-crushers wrong.

Don't waste time trying to change or arguing with them.

"Never argue with a fool, onlookers may not be able to tell the difference." – Mark Twain

Just surround yourself with like-minded educators, tread your own path and change the world.

The five people you spend the most time with are a great indicator of who you are . . . so avoid negative people.

DESIGN MATTERS

As educators, we wear many hats.

 Teacher.
 Police officer.
 Doctor.
 Therapist.

One hat many teachers don't wear often enough is designer.

Our job relies on engaging and communicating with an audience.

Big companies spend millions to engage and communicate with their audience because they know they have to look good to win an audience's attention.

Obviously, we can't spend the dollars of the big companies, but we can copy them.

Imagine if Nike, X-Box or Coke made teaching resources; what would they look like?

Taking a few extra minutes to consider how things (posters, forms, worksheets, etc.) are designed will likely lead to greater engagement from your students.

STUDY GREAT TEACHERS AND THEIR IMPACT

As a new teacher, I used to sit in other teachers' classrooms just to learn from them.

I saw them motivate, inspire, direct and discipline their students.

Much of what is in this book comes from those early days of studying great teachers and figuring out how they had such a positive impact on their students.

It is an investment of valuable time, especially for a new teacher, but it will pay massive dividends in the long run.

As early as possible, find a mentor that teaches in a way you'd like to teach, and ask if you can sit in his or her class and learn.

TRAFFIC FLOW

Often, classroom behaviour issues can be improved when traffic flow improves.

Rather than have all your students huddling around one area, here are a few options . . .

- Spread the resources around the room in different stations.
- Ask one person to collect resources for five people.
- Already have the resources where the students will be working (on their table).

This obviously applies to all teaching, whether sports equipment in a physical education lesson or books/iPads in a classroom.

Another area that is a "breeding ground for trouble" is the bag room/locker area.

Personally, I give kids their own bag hook/area, and they are placed strategically to try to separate personality clashes.

Students are also sent to get their bags in smaller groups to avoid congestion.

TEACHABLE MOMENTS

Keep your eyes out for amazing teachable moments.

My best teaching is usually unplanned, which might also say something about my planning.

One of my favourite lessons was when I accidentally left a bottle of orange juice at school . . . over the holidays.

> The top of the bottle shot off and made a dent in the roof.
> The OJ fizzed out of the bottle and exploded like champagne.
> The smell of alcohol filled the classroom.
> We headed off down the path of fermentation and chemical change.

I now ferment orange juice and other liquids with my students at the start of every year as a hook. Students aren't used to having a winery in their classroom.

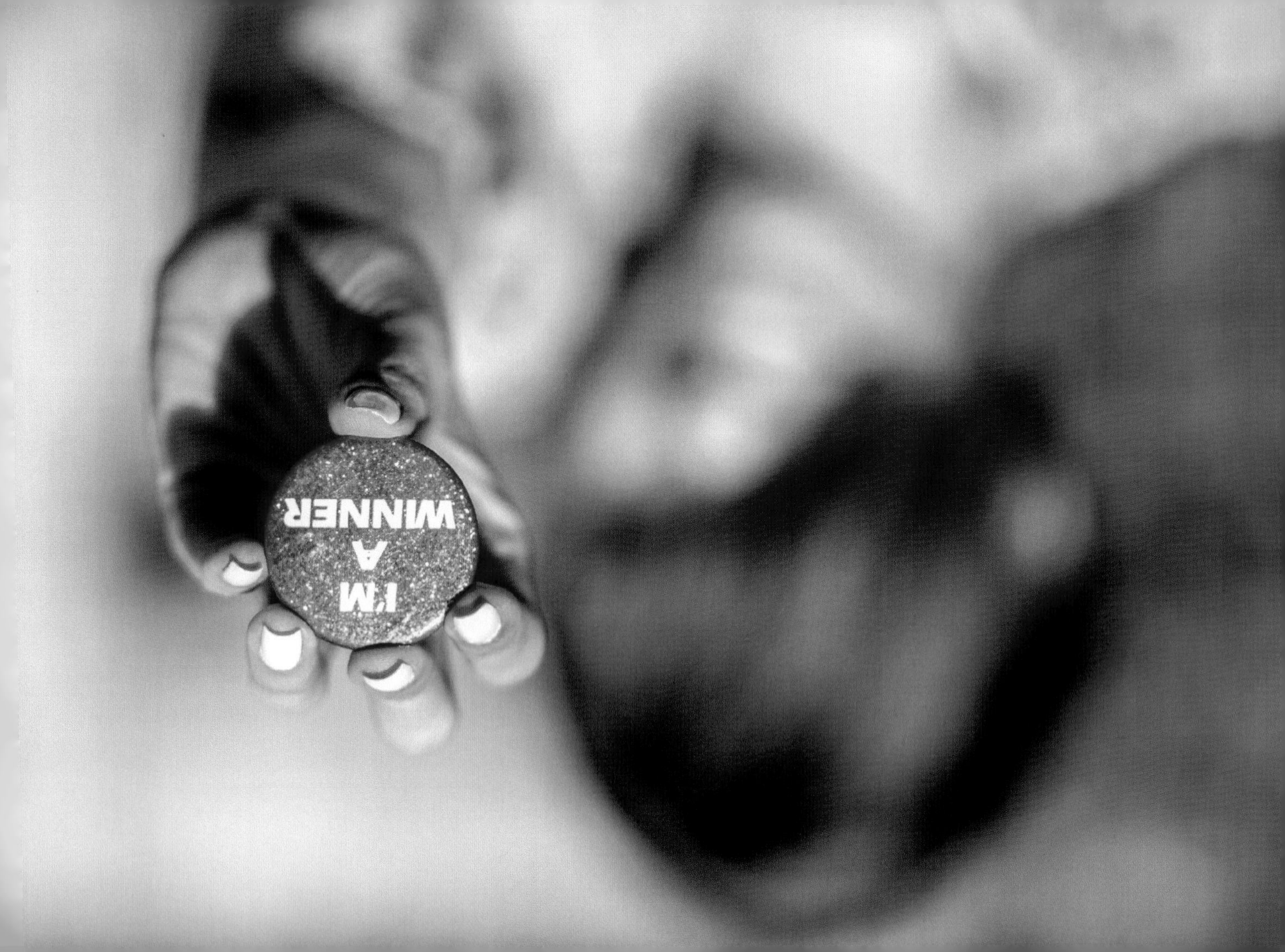
I'M
A
WINNER

PRAISE BEHAVIOUR OVER PRODUCT

"I'm impressed by your attention to detail on your presentation" is much better than "Pretty handwriting".

We want kids to value the process as much as, if not more than, the product. Therefore, as teachers, we must value the process.

It's not to say you can't comment on the product, but where possible, it should be linked to the process.

"I can clearly see you have put a lot of thought into your planning because this is a well-constructed story."

"Your effort today, even though you weren't sure of the answer, has been outstanding. That's the stuff that makes people successful."

Education systems are often built around students trying to please, or appease, their teachers.

Personally, I want my students to aim to please themselves, not me.

This structure is more sustainable for a classroom and the real world.

By focusing on the learning and not the product we encourage students to be more reflective and see the value they have gained.

Student: "How's this, Mr. Bowman?"
Teacher: "I'm impressed, but more importantly, how do *you* feel about it?"

or

Teacher: "Well, it looks cool to me, but what did you get out of doing it/what did you learn?"

Obvious, yeah?

It gives your voice a rest.

It makes learning interactive.

T: *What do you think about X?*
T: *Why do you think that?*
T: *How about if it was upside down/older/blue/whatever?*

It gives you feedback on your teaching and their learning.

T: *Could someone please explain X in their own words?*

It makes kids think and engage their processing brain.

S: *Can I please get a drink/use coloured markers?*
T: *What's in it for me?*

This makes students use empathy and justification.

It keeps kids "on their toes" because they may be asked.

Have a container with all your students' names in it and draw from it to decide who answers the question. This leads on to . . .

AVOID "NO" AND "WRONG"

When a student gives an incorrect answer, avoid a hard "no" or "wrong" at all costs.

These responses are embarrassing to the student and mean it will be less likely they contribute an answer again.

Instead, try to search for a positive from their answer or help them to find the answer.

"I can see why you might think that but . . ."
"That's an interesting idea; I hadn't thought about it that way . . ."
"Not quite, but I can see you're on the right track . . ."
"You know what, your answer is a bit off . . . but I love the way you approach these problems."
"That's a good idea, but what would happen if you included/thought of this . . ."
"Yeah . . . that is a great idea and very close, but not quite what I'm after . . . clever thinking, though."

TEACHING MANNERS

Basic manners include:

- Being an active listener.
- Taking turns.
- Opening the door for others.
- Offering help.
- Making eye contact.
- Being on time or apologising if late.
- Saying "please" and "thank you".

These are not an exceptional requirement.

They are the minimal requirement.

If we do not explicitly teach our students manners, we are doing them a great disservice.

Once again, the best way to teach manners is to model them.

FOCUS ON THE JOURNEY

"It's not where you start that matters. It's where you finish."

I have this quote split in half (start/finish) on opposite sides of my classroom, and it's joined by a piece of string that zigzags all over my classroom.

I constantly refer to it, so my students are reminded they shouldn't compare themselves to one another; they should compare themselves to where they were yesterday or last month.

Focusing on the journey encourages students to focus on the next step, rather than where they sit in regards to others.

LET KIDS DISLIKE YOU

When I "tell a kid off", I give him or her permission to dislike me.

Explicitly letting a student know he or she can dislike you does two things:

It surprises the student.
"You probably don't like me right now, and that's OK" is not something most students hear from their teachers, and as a result, it makes them recalibrate.

It defuses the situation.
Acknowledging and allowing a student to feel upset instantly makes you more aligned with the student, and they relax a little. "I understand if you don't like me right now, but I hope that in the future you will understand I did this because I wanted to teach you that your behaviour was unacceptable to me and to others. But, at the moment, I'm OK if you'd rather just be annoyed at me."

STUDENT BAROMETERS

Student barometers are a great indicator of how a lesson is going.

It might be a different kid depending on what you're trying to get feedback on.

I certainly have different kids I use to look for cues on how my teaching is progressing.

The cues might be visual, such as how a student is sitting (forward in chair, leaning back, head on desk, etc.), or you might just ask a student.

>"Am I talking too much?"
>"Was that fair?"
>"How long is that going to take you?"

You can take or leave their feedback, but it is often good to get a student's perspective and then re-calibrate.

10,000 STEPS PER DAY

I love asking kids, "What makes a good teacher?"

Every time someone says, "They don't sit behind their desk all day."

Moving around the classroom helps prevent "spot fires" and allows teachers to have a much better idea of where their students are at, academically and emotionally.

Nowadays, pedometers are cheap and available all over, so I'd recommend grabbing one and checking out your step count.

As a bonus, the World Health Organisation recommends that people walk 10,000 steps per day for good health . . . Why not do it at work and get paid for it?

BE ON TIME

This is really obvious, but sadly, it is a very common problem.

Being on time is important for three reasons:

It's your **legal responsibility**, your duty of care. If you're not there when you should be, you can get in *big* trouble.

It shows students that we **value their learning time**.

If we're late, it says the opposite.

Kids left unattended with nothing to do often equals trouble (e.g., Lord of the Flies). Just by being on time, it is possible to reduce incidents between students.

BUILD UP ONE LESSON AT A TIME

The best advice I got at university from a lecture was to make one great lesson per day (even every second day).

The rest of your lessons should be good, but focus on making one *great*.

Then, next year you'll have that great lesson, and you can make another one.

In a few years, you will have a week's worth of amazing lessons.

If you try to do too much from the start, the chances are things, or you, will come crashing down at some point.

AVOIDING CONFLICT

You're teaching a class, and a rather challenging student is playing with a toy car and distracting others.

You have two options:

"Put your (toy) car in your bag please, Tom."

OR

"Wow, that looks awesome, Tom. Is it a Ferrari? Do you mind if I have a look at it after class? In the meantime, can you please pop it in your bag and help me get this organised?"

This happened to me, and I chose option one.

Tom became defiant and violent; then my principal had to be called up to fix the situation.

My principal, who had cleaned up the mess I had created, taught me option two . . . which I've used a lot since.

ONE MINUTE PER YEAR

As a *very* rough guide, think about your students' attention span being their age.

    5-year-old = 5 minutes of concentration.

    13-year-old = 13 minutes of concentration.

    94-year-old = . . . OK, the guide probably isn't that specific.

AIM TO BECOME REDUNDANT

As a teacher, my goal is to become redundant . . . to my students, not my school.

I want students to value my help and support but not to need it.

My goal is to develop my students so that they can solve their own problems, make their own decisions and treat people how they would like to be treated.

I get a big kick out of receiving positive feedback about my students when I'm not there.

Obviously, the level of independence you can expect from a student varies on their age, but push students to become independent and not need you.

LOOK PAST THE PROBLEM TO THE SOLUTION

The first step to students becoming independent is creating problem solvers.

When students come to you with a problem, ask them to come up with their request/solution instead.

- I need to wee → Can I please go to the toilet?
- My iPad is flat → Can I please borrow the iPad charger?
- He pushed me → Can I please go to the sick bay? Can you please speak to that boy about playing fairly?
- No one will play with me → How can I find someone to play with?

Sometimes this may feel harsh, but by teaching a student how to solve their own problems, you are teaching them a skill for life.

> *"Give a man a fish and you feed him for a day; teach a man to fish and you feed him for a lifetime."*

SMALL AND FAST, TO MAKE BIG AND LONG

Rather than setting one big, long task, think about breaking it into smaller, faster tasks.

I often do fast/rocket writing with my students.

I show them a prompt, usually an image, and give them a very short amount of time (1–4 min) to write about it. They then share their writing by reading it aloud to the person next to them, or the class if they like, and we move on to another prompt.

After half a dozen prompts even the most reluctant writers have written more than they could have imagined. If I had asked them to write about one prompt for the same amount of time the results would likely be very different.

By breaking down tasks, they become much more manageable for students. I have found this applies to almost anything . . . for any age.

Bonus tip: By putting a box around a question, it gives many kids a sense of security. They can see the end and know what is expected.

WHOM DO YOU ANSWER TO?

As a teacher, whom do we answer to?

Minister for Education?
Principal?
Students?
Parents?
Ourselves?

The answer I've come up with is the students as they are now, and where they'll be in a week, month, year, five years' and twenty years' time.

If I teach to develop my students' attitude, skills and knowledge that will best equip them for the future, I feel I can sleep at night.

Whom do you answer to?

HOW TO GET A JOB ... ADD VALUE

To get the job you want, you must show "added value".

There are a lot of teachers applying for the same job, so what do you offer a school that other teachers don't?

Can you choreograph the school production?
Can you run a human-powered vehicle team?
Can you design the school website?
Can you coach a sports team?
Can you . . . whatever!

The more you can offer a school, the greater your chances of getting the job you want.

Therefore, the sooner you start to fill your CV with offers (things you can do), the better position you'll be in when you apply for your next job.

ASK THREE, THEN ASK ME

"Ask three, then ask me" is a way to assist students to solve their own problems and free you up.

Students must ask three students for help in the following order, before they ask the teacher for help.

Ask yourself – Have you really tried to fix it yourself?

Ask a friend – Ask a person near you.

Ask an expert – Whom might be an "expert" that could help you solve this problem?

Then ask the teacher – When a student comes up to ask a question, simply ask, "Have you asked three?"

If they have asked three, you can ask who they were, or get on with helping.

If they haven't, you can send them away or help them with whom to ask.

THEY'RE ONLY KIDS

Once, I was frustrated at my students for not being as mature as I'd like.

They weren't listening; they were messing around and wasting time.

I spoke to a colleague and shared my frustration.

"Don't forget . . . they're only kids. They're nine years old," said my colleague.

Kids are not "little adults", and we shouldn't expect them to behave like they are.

Kids can be impulsive, lacking in focus, silly and easily distracted.

Their job is to be a kid.

Our job is to help them learn and grow over time.

HAVE A BAG OF TRICKS

With the Internet, there is no excuse for not having a bag of tricks (a handful of activities you can run without time or resources).

Some of the best "tricks" I have, or have seen are:

- Magic tricks (I use the "Disappearing Coin" trick).
- Logic problems/riddles/philosophy questions.
- Songs (if you can sing and play an instrument, I envy you).
- Games (cards, dice, ball games, etc.).
- Creative challenges.
- Drama activities.
- Truth or lie?: Tell them ten things about you (five are true/lies), and they have pick which ones are true/lies. Then they have a turn at telling me something about them and I try and guess if it is a truth or lie.
- Philosophy questions: "If you caught someone cheating on a test, would you dob them in? What if they were your best friend? What if the test was for one spot, that you *really* wanted, and they were going to take it over you? What if you'd also been cheating but hadn't been caught?"

BETTER TOO MUCH THAN TOO LITTLE

When I started out, I always over-planned.

One day's planning would turn out to be three days' worth.

I was fine with that, because it's much better to have too much to do than too little, especially when starting out.

When you're starting out, it's incredibly difficult to know how long to set aside for activities.

You don't know the kids, and you don't know the tasks.

It's always better to run out of time and come back to something, rather than be left drowning, trying to fill in time.

RANDOM SEATS FOR STUDENTS

I love giving kids random seats in class.

I print their names off and draw their seat out of a hat.

I feel it simulates real life.

Very rarely do employees get to choose who they work with.

Learning to co-operate with a diverse range of people is one of the most important skills a student will learn at school.

Sometimes, I leave the seating arrangement for three weeks, other times I reallocated them after 90 minutes.

DON'T MISS AN OPPORTUNITY

There was a teacher of a "challenging kid". They often clashed.

One day, they'd been at a sports event, and the boy had left his jumper behind. He was terribly upset and in tears because his mum was going to be angry.

It was the end of the day, the bell had gone. He needed to make a phone call and the teacher sent him to the office. To me, it was a missed opportunity.

The boy was in a vulnerable state and needed help.

He had no idea how to deal with the situation.

There would never have been a better opportunity for the teacher to establish a relationship of trust between the two.

But the teacher missed it by sending him away rather than giving him the extra four minutes to talk through a strategy and allow him to call from the classroom phone.

Their year continued to be a battle, and I often wonder how things could have been different.

YOU ARE NOT "JUST A TEACHER"

I used to feel, and sometimes still do, like I'm "just a teacher".

I think it's the social stigma that "Those that can, do; those that can't, teach".

One day, I was talking to a friend who I respected greatly for his professional accomplishments of being a well-respected medical doctor.

I used the phrase, "I'm just a teacher". He set me straight.

Teachers, especially good ones, are incredibly important.

Without that doctor's great teachers, he wouldn't be doing what he does . . . saving lives.

The impact of a great educator can extend across generations.

"You can count the apples on a tree but you can't count the trees from one apple."

In the day-to-day grind of teaching, it is easy to forget how truly important you are.

You are important.

You matter.

How you teach matters.

So get your skates on and change the world!

THE LAST ONE

All these are ideas, *not* rules.

Break them, bend them and test them.

Most importantly . . .

Give your students chocolate and free time! (Refer to #1.)

About the author – Tim Bowman

I'm a teacher . . . because I had nothing else on offer.

After three years studying to become an actor, and not becoming Hugh Jackman, my parents convinced/pushed me to study teaching.

I didn't like studying teaching at uni. It seemed so dry and teaching rounds/ placements terrified me. The thought of having my own class . . . no, thank you.

Then I began teaching, and I fell in love with it. I truly believe it is an amazing profession whereby you can change the world, learn how to be a better parent to your own kids (if you choose to be a parent), get paid and have awesome holidays.

I've been fortunate enough to work at a variety of schools, teaching a variety of age groups and subjects. I've also worked in Hong Kong, teaching in local and international schools. Teaching overseas is certainly an experience I would recommend to any teacher, especially young ones. I really learnt to teach when I was in charge of a class of forty preps who didn't speak my language.

In 2015 I took the year off to write this book and develop some educational software (Class Creator https://www.classcreator.io/). The best thing about being out of the classroom for a year, apart from being with my family, has been realising how much I love it.

Thank you for checking out my book, and good luck with all things education.

Cheers,
Tim
tim@classcreator.io
www.facebook.com/88ideasteaching/
Twitter: @TimBowman14

Also check out
I've loved learning about education from a lot of sources.
Here are a few I would recommend you check out:

John Hattie
"Know thy impact"
Mr Visible Learning
http://visiblelearningplus.com/

James Nottingham
"Students we want the least, need us the most"
Mr Learning Pit
http://www.jamesnottingham.co.uk/

Todd Whitaker –
"Students we want the least, need us the most"
Mr Lots of Stuff
http://www.toddwhitaker.com/

TED
Ideas worth sharing.
https://www.ted.com/

Sir Ken Robinsion
"Imagination is the source of all human achievement"
Mr Creative Schools
http://sirkenrobinson.com/

Bill Rogers
"Students we want the least, need us the most"
Mr Behaviour Management
http://www.billrogers.com.au/

Seth Godin
"The only thing worse than starting something and failing . . . is not starting something.
Mr Make Something Happen
http://www.sethgodin.com

Gary Vaynerchuk
"Hustle"
Mr Hustle. An example of passion, engaging an audience and keeping it real.
https://www.garyvaynerchuk.com/

Ken Watanabe
Problem Solving 101: A Simple Book for Smart People
Mr Problem Solving
http://www.amazon.com/Problem-Solving-101-Simple-People/dp/1591842425

Freakonomics – Steven Levitt & Stephen Dubner
Mr & Mr Freakonomics
http://freakonomics.com/

Malcolm Gladwell
Author of cool ideas and observations
http://gladwell.com/

Tim Ferris
"No work for works' sake"
Mr Four Hour Work Week
http://gladwell.com/